Junior Year is the Key to Homeschool Success

How to Unlock the Gate to Graduation and Beyond

Lee Binz,
The HomeScholar

First Printing, 2014

Printed in the United States of America

ISBN: 1502464918
ISBN-13: 978-1502464910

Disclaimer: Parents assume full responsibility for the education of their children in accordance with state law. College requirements vary, so make sure to check with the colleges about specific requirements for homeschoolers. We offer no guarantees, written or implied, that the use of our products and services will result in college admissions or scholarship awards.

Junior Year is the Key to Homeschool Success

How to Unlock the Gate to Graduation and Beyond

What are Coffee Break Books?

"Junior Year is the Key to Homeschool Success" is part of The HomeScholar's Coffee Break Book series.

Designed especially for parents who don't want to spend hours and hours reading a 400-page book on homeschooling high school, each book combines Lee's practical and friendly approach with detailed, but easy-to-digest information, perfect to read over a cup of coffee at your favorite coffee shop!

Never overwhelming, always accessible and manageable, each book in the series will give parents the tools they need to tackle the tasks of homeschooling high school, one warm sip at a time.

Everything about these Coffee Break Books is designed to suggest simplicity, ease and comfort; from the size (fits in a purse), to the font and paragraph length (easy on the eyes), to the price (the same as a Starbucks Venti Triple Caramel Macchiato). Unlike a fancy coffee drink, however, these books are guilt-free pleasures you will want to enjoy again and again!

Table of Contents

Introduction

Game On

If your homeschool student plans to attend college after graduation, junior year is their most important year of high school. If you've "dropped the ball" the previous years, there is still time to catch up and be ready for college applications during senior year. If you've kept good records all along and given your child a college prep education, there are still plenty of other things that need to be done, so being prepared is the key. College preparation can be pretty stressful, for both student and parent, and staying on top of all the key components will be very important.

In this book, we'll cover the important tasks of junior year, including preparing for and taking college admissions tests, attending college fairs, choosing a college, finding merit scholarships, and how to get a jump on senior year.

Both parents and teens have a job to do during junior year. Teens need to work hard, both academically and by volunteering or working. Parents need to prepare high school records, manage the big picture project of high school graduation and college admissions, and help their child with the college search process.

As a parent, you are the best guidance counselor for your child, because the best guidance counselor loves your child, understands your family finances, and appreciates your family goals. No one does these things better than you! There are certain tasks that a guidance counselor does. These include researching college admissions, reading about colleges, looking online for resources, and preparing your high school records. To be honest, most of that isn't difficult! Sure, preparing homeschool records is time consuming, but it's not hard; the key to preparing your records is to do it every year.

The first step is to plan your child's high school classes. During junior year, make sure that you complete the necessary core classes; junior year is the critical time to fill in any gaps that you see. Make sure to maintain balance, and don't try to fit four years of high school into one year. Schedule your classes so that your child can cover what they need each year, but make sure that by junior year you have identified any gaps. For instance, if you haven't started a foreign language by junior year, that is a gap, so start making a plan to fill any gaps as you plan your courses.

Plan for college tests as well. It's important that your student have some practice at tests, that you register on time, that you understand and use the results, and send the scores where they're needed.

You also have to organize a college search. Try not to decide that your child is just going to apply to a school that's close to you, because this will not always result in good scholarship money. Organize a college search by going to college fairs and doing some research.

Lastly, make sure to review all the portions of the college applications, as that will help you understand what you need to do. Although junior year can seem overwhelming, if you are armed with a good plan and the knowledge you need, college admissions and scholarships will be your reward.

Start now, and get ready for success!

Chapter 1

Parent Tasks During Junior Year

During junior year, there are tasks that are specific for parents. Obviously, there are some jobs that you'll do which are more "counselor" jobs, and some jobs that are more parent jobs. Balancing your family values with career plans and financial obligations are an example of parent tasks. For example, your child might want to be an engineer, but you are committed to not having a huge financial burden, and you want to see your child go to a Christian engineering school. The bottom line is that although you can provide a wide array of options for your child, if you as the parent write the check, it's really the parent that gets to decide.

Make sure to consider college financing, and save money for college. Work to position your student for scholarships, since junior year is a really good time to look for private scholarships.

Plan Classes

When planning classes for junior year, make sure that you cover the core. During high school you need four English classes, four Math classes, four Social Studies, and at least three Sciences. To get there, you will need to pretty much cover these topics each year. Remember that you can't cover four years of high school English in three years. Make a plan so that you're sure you've got three credits done by junior year, and plan to catch that last credit of English, math and social studies during senior year.

Fill any gaps. The usual gaps that I see are foreign language, which can be a hurdle for people to overcome. Once you make that jump and start to study foreign language, it's not so hard, but to me it felt like upper math. It was a scary subject for me, but once you start, then it's not so bad.

The other thing to pay attention to is Fine Art, because only one credit is required. If your child is really good at the fine arts, you'll have a lot of credits in that area. But if they're not, then sometimes it's forgotten, and sometimes that can be one of those gaps that need to be filled.

Plan Electives

During junior year, don't forget to plan electives. One source of elective credit is the delight directed learning that your child does for fun. If your child does modeling for Nordstrom's, and it's what they do for fun, then you can collect those as their elective credits. You can collect credits from family requirements. If your family requires Bible instruction or home economics, those family requirements are a source of electives as well.

Finally, you can collect your electives because of state law. In Washington State, we are required to teach occupational education. It's required by state law, but it doesn't fit anywhere else, so it's an elective. Find out what your state requires, and see whether those will count as electives for you.

Plan to Take the PSAT

Plan to take the PSAT in October of junior year. Register early, but be aware that some schools register in May or June, and other schools register in September. There are also some schools that actually allow you to walk-in to take the test, which is pretty unusual, but it can happen. Check your calendar and make sure that you plan and register early to take that test. In general if you call your local high school in June, they can help you figure it out. Put the registration date on the calendar and make sure that you register on time.

I suggest that you take the PSAT in junior year. I also think it's very helpful if you take the PSAT during sophomore year. It can help you practice how to register for the test, and it can help you reduce the fear in your student.

There are some kids that have some testing anxiety, and taking it for fun when it doesn't count in 10th grade can take the mystique out of it. It can help young people to overcome any fear of sitting in a strange school cafeteria with people that they don't know. Because they'll probably take the test in the same place year after year, it will help them feel more familiar with the location. Practice makes perfect, and I recommend that you take the PSAT in 10th grade just for fun, and then take it in 11th grade when it counts for real.

Practice the PSAT

Speaking of practice, it is a good idea to practice for the PSAT. Go over the sample PSAT test they'll give you when you register. Take that sample test and practice with it, even the non-test portion. There is a huge part in the front, where they don't ask any test questions, where your child will have to fill in their name, grade in school, number of classes they've taken, etc. Those non-test portions are sometimes harder for homeschoolers to answer than the test questions, since it asks about classes and grades that homeschoolers don't usually talk to their children about.

Make sure to show your child their transcript before they take the PSAT, so that they know how many classes they've taken and what grade they're in. In the non-test portion, they'll also ask about college choices, and whether you want your scores reported to any schools. It's really important for you to go over even the non-test portion of the PSAT, just for practice.

Before you take the test, locate your homeschool code. You can do it the hard way, which is to do a Google search for "PSAT/NMSQT Codes for Home-Schooled Students", or you can go to www.collegeboard.com/student/testing/psat/reg/homeschool/state-codes.html, which is more direct. The code for each state is different, which is why I can't tell you what your code is – you have to look it up for your individual state.

The PSAT presents a wonderful opportunity for a diversity discussion with your student, prior to taking the test.

We live in an inner-city area, and our local high school has a 46% drop out rate. It was a pretty sketchy environment and when my kids were in the public school cafeteria with around 500 other kids while taking the PSAT, they noticed that there was a lot of sneezing, snorting, swearing, and tattoos. It was a wonderful opportunity to discuss why we are thankful to homeschool. For Christian teens, I think it's a good opportunity to discuss John 3:16 "For God so loved the world..." and not just the conservatively dressed world.

Test Day Strategies

The best thing you can do for your child on test day is to make sure they are not running on empty. Make sure they get plenty of sleep, at least the night before, and preferably two weeks before. On the day of the test, make sure they get a good breakfast with protein, and take a snack and water or juice with them when they go to the test. Take a calculator they feel comfortable using.

Make sure they bring their homeschool code with them. Usually the test proctors will give you the code, but sometimes they get confused and it takes a few minutes for them to look it up. For that reason, it can reduce the stress level of your child if they know what their test code is.

Most importantly, locate the bathrooms! Chances are, your child does not know where the bathroom is in the high school cafeteria, so help them find it. I know one student who raised his score by 200 points per section simply by knowing where the bathroom was the second time around!

Also plan a pickup location ahead of time, because they'll want to know where you're going to find them afterwards. Sometimes they'll say the test will end at a certain time, but then it will go later than everyone thinks. Be prepared, and your children will be more comfortable, which means they will be better able to do their best!

For more information about the PSAT, see Appendix 1: **Take the PSAT for Fun and Profit.**

Chapter 2

College Admission Tests

One of the big jobs during junior year is to decide whether your child will take the SAT or the ACT. Give a timed sample of both at home, and then compare the scores by percentile. The SAT scores are 200-800 per section. The ACT scores range from 1 to 36. You really can't compare scores to scores, so just look at the percentile scores and compare those.

Choose the test that is best for your child, and have them study for that test. Girls often score better on the ACT and boys on the SAT; science-loving kids often score better on the ACT. Both tests have an optional essay, as well, so if your child is not a strong writer, they might do better without the essay. Most colleges require the optional essay, so even though the test might say the essay is optional, colleges will say it is required. Make sure you understand what your college wants before skipping the optional essay.

Study for the SAT or ACT

Once you have determined which test is better for your child, have them start to study. Study for the test that is the best fit for your child. Not everybody will study exactly the same, but I usually recommend studying 3 to 5 times per week, each time for about 30 minutes. That means you do one section of the test, which is timed so you get timed practice.

Correct the test and spend about ten minutes or so reviewing wrong answers. There's no point reviewing the right answers! Review the explanations so they understand why they got them wrong. That's usually the quickest and easiest way to improve.

I do a lot of reading on SAT prep materials, and I've found the Princeton Review materials are a little more accessible for teenagers than Kaplan, REA or Peterson's. I found those to be a bit boring, but Princeton Review was interesting, and they use real SAT questions.

If your child needs a lot of help to take a test, then "Cracking the SAT" or "Cracking the ACT" would be a good book to help them prepare. If your child is beyond that and is ready to practice with more tests, then I recommend you get the "Princeton Review 11 Real Practice Tests" or the "Princeton Review Real Practice Test for the ACT."

Test Prep on the Transcript

One of the great things about test prep is that you can put it on your child's transcript. If your child spends half an hour a day most of the school year on test prep, that equals a half credit class, which you could call Study Skills. On average, 120-180 hours makes a whole credit, or studying for a whole hour a day most of the school year also equals a credit. Generally speaking, most students will earn half a credit for studying. You can add other study skills, such as note-taking, together with your test prep and build it up to a one-credit class if you like.

You can also replace some of your grade level work books with test preparation books. If you spend any time on "Worldly Wise" or a spelling book, your test preparation could replace vocabulary and spelling, or your math review or grammar review. The writing that you do once a week with your test prep could replace the composition that you do that day.

Take Admission Tests

I recommend taking admission tests in March of junior year, if possible. When you take the SAT or the ACT in March, that gives you time to see the results, which should arrive about two weeks later. This will allow you to repeat the test if you need to. You could take the SAT in March, look at the results, study a bit more, and take the test again in May. It's still junior year, you're not behind, there's no stress at all. Unless your student scores exceedingly well, I suggest that people take either the SAT or the ACT twice. In fact, there are some colleges that actually want you to take the test twice.

Some colleges will even ask you to take both the SAT and ACT! They want kids that are smart and have good tests scores, because those raise the value of the college. If you take a test twice, a school will sometimes choose the best score and give you more scholarship money. You'll make their school look good, because your child comes to college with higher test scores. On the other hand, there are quite a few colleges that will discourage you from taking the test three times. Twice is good, but three times is not good, so don't take it a third time unless critical for admission.

If your child takes the test one time as a junior, they can still repeat the test during senior year, but only if necessary. You need the test results in order to move forward during senior year, since they will help you figure out what is the right college to apply to. That's why it's important to take it during junior year, so that you can make those decisions about college when your student becomes a senior.

For more information on this topic, see my Coffee Break Book, "High School Testing: Knowledge That Saves Money."

Chapter 3

Teach Quick Essay Skills

One of the most significant parts of the SAT and ACT is the quick essay, which is timed essay. Your student will have a few minutes to read the topic, quickly make an outline of two or three things they intend to say, and then write the essay. It's challenging, and it's one of the reasons why you want to practice it before you take the test for real. The essay is optional on the SAT and ACT.

Practicing quick essays skills can help you document other classes as well. Base the writing topic on whatever is the focus of your child's delight directed learning. For instance, if your child gives swim lessons to children, then have them write a quick essay on that. Or use the quick essay to document other classes, like the Bible course they've been doing. This essay can help you provide some work samples for classes that don't have any tests involved. If you use a history curriculum that doesn't have tests, your child can write a quick essay about some topic in their history class.

A quick essay prepares children for college classes, because it's something that they will run into frequently at college. One of the reasons why colleges love homeschoolers is that they know how to write a quick essay. Experience writing essays can also make your student's college applications less stressful, because they will already know how to write an essay when they're under pressure. Just treat the application essays as a quick essay, and before you know it, they'll be done.

Of everything I taught my children, the one thing my son actually came back to thank me for was teaching him how to write a quick essay. Within a month or two of starting college, he took his first essay test. He was one of the very few students in the class who didn't panic and was very glad he learned how to write in high school. Make sure your child learns these skills too, and perhaps they will come back to thank you!

For more information on this topic, see my Coffee Break Book, "Easy English for Simple Homeschooling: How to Teach, Assess and Document High School English."

Chapter 4

Subject Tests

During junior year, consider having your student take some subject tests. These are tests that only measure one subject at a time, such as a test of economics or chemistry. Subject tests don't test multiple skills like the SAT or ACT. Check the requirements of the colleges where your student plans to apply. See whether they require or accept subject tests. Take subject tests in the spring after the subject is completed, while the information is still fresh in your student's mind.

In some situations, it's important to exceed the requirements of a college. If you need a lot of scholarships, take multiple subject tests and exceed the requirements, so that your child will look especially good. This is important, especially if you apply to very selective schools. If they say they don't require subject tests but everyone else has those qualifications, your student will look better if they have those tests too. Find out what the colleges want and then give it to them, so that your student has a higher chance of winning scholarships.

Choose Subject Tests

You can find information about subject tests on the College Board website, www.collegeboard.com. The SAT subject tests are high school level tests in one single subject area, taken at a local high school. It's a fill-in the bubble type of test.

The AP subject tests are college level tests, which are taken at a local high school as well. The content of the AP is taken from standardized coursework. While no specific textbooks are required, knowledge of the content of the class is required in order to do well. Although there are some fill-in-the-blank questions, the AP is primarily an essay test.

College Level Examination Program (CLEP) subject tests are college level tests in a single subject area. These tests are usually given at community colleges and technical colleges. Check the college policies of the schools you're interested in, since some colleges accept CLEP and others won't.

Take Subject Tests

Register for subject tests early, and take the test when your student has completed the subject, usually in the spring when they've completed the course. Take multiple practice tests at home, so your student really understands the test inside and out. As much as possible, make sure that your student will be able to pass the test before they take it for real.

Before your student takes the test, they must decide to either have their scores sent directly to the schools they're interested in, or to have them withheld until later. This allows you to see what they get on the test before you decide to send them to the schools. Waiting to send the scores is usually a more expensive option, since they'll charge you to hold the scores and submit them later. It's less expensive to wait on taking the test until you're very sure that your child is going to do well, and then have them sent automatically to the colleges.

Chapter 5

Three Steps to Finding a College

There are three steps to choosing a college that's a good fit. Each step requires an investment of your time, money, and coordination.

First, find a college you would like to visit by attending a college fair. Second, make an official visit at the colleges where you might be interested. Third, use the information you have collected to choose at least a handful of appropriate colleges to apply to. Let me explain how it works.

STEP ONE: ATTEND A COLLEGE FAIR

Are you going to your State Fair? In the Pacific Northwest where I live, fall is fair time. My family looks forward to seeing the animals, riding the crazy rides, and eating the great fair food! It's all a lot of fun. But state fairs aren't the only fairs in the fall. It's also college fair season and they are even more important for high school students and parents.

Efficient Evaluation

Attending a college fair is the most effective and efficient way to come up with a list of potential colleges to consider. Instead of traveling all over the country to visit different schools, they all come to you! You'll find all sorts of colleges in one convenient location. If you're looking for that 'perfect fit' college for your high school student, look no further than your closest college fair to begin your search. Even for those who live a little too far away from a big city to make a day trip possible, it's worth the investment to travel to your closest city to attend a fair, even if it takes a day or two. The opportunity to find out about so many schools in one location is really worth the time and money.

Booths and Workshops

College fairs are a lot like your typical homeschool convention. The company comes to you! You'll see lots of booths, workshops, people, noise, and hard concrete floors. However, instead of homeschool curriculum, the product being sold is a college education. In addition to colleges, you will find other companies and organizations affiliated with college admission and scholarships, such as The Princeton Review, the College Board, and others like them. Stop by their booths and pick up their free samples! Take classes on different topics related to college admission and scholarships. These might include seminars on SAT preparation, financial aid, college life, admissions, etc. These are worth attending, as the more you know about these topics, the better prepared you will be to help your student succeed.

Finding a Fair

Homeschoolers who live close to a large city should have an easy time finding a college fair nearby. If you search online for 'college fair' and the name of your city, you will probably find several options. In addition, there are larger fairs put on by private organizations each year. The biggest are the National Association for College Admission Counseling (nacacnet.org), and the North American Coalition for Christian Admissions Professionals (naccap.org). There are also specialized groups that have fairs. Exploring College Options Consortium represents Ivy League schools (exploringcollegeoptions.org), Colleges That Change Lives (ctcl.org), Historically Black Colleges and Universities (hbcufair.com) and Performing and Visual Arts fairs.

Students First

College fairs are for students and parents. Students need to ask questions and explore possibilities; they need to introduce themselves to representatives of schools, and find out whether a school has what they think they need—whether that's a swimming pool, a French major, or pizza in the cafeteria. Encourage your student to be conversational and friendly in their interactions, and to dress neatly and cleanly for the day. Parents have important questions too! What is the college's homeschool policy? Do they accept CLEP or AP credits? Do they offer whopping big financial aid?! What are the average SAT/ACT test scores for this school? These questions will help you determine whether a school will be a good fit for your student.

Parents Second

Financial aid is a topic on many parents' minds as they wander through the aisles of a college fair. Fortunately, a college fair is a great place to find a school that will offer your child assistance. Most schools are pretty up front about what they're looking for in an applicant; find one that's looking for what your student has, and you may find some pretty attractive financial aid. And it's not always academic accomplishment they're looking for. At one college fair I attended, I overhead a school representative say they were looking for a student from Nebraska, so they could say they had a representative from every state in the union. You can imagine what good scholarship money they were offering to any Nebraskan applicant! Another school I know of offered a great scholarship to an applicant who was an accomplished pianist, because their choir really needed an accompanist. If you find a few schools you're interested in at the fair, be sure to ask them what they're looking for from their applicants, and see whether your student just might fit the bill.

Online Option

If you simply can't make it to a college fair, don't despair; there are a few other options. The College Board (www.collegeboard.com) has a very user-friendly college search program, and other resources like Fastweb and US News and World Report can help you find colleges that match your student's interests and abilities. If your child will take the PSAT soon, have them check the college search box to receive college information, and colleges who are interested in your student will send you admission information. Even though online searches are very helpful, they can't replace attending a college fair. Typically dozens, and sometimes hundreds of schools are represented at a fair, and nothing beats a face-to-face encounter with a representative who is familiar with their school. In addition to attending a fair, educate yourself as much as possible about the college admission and scholarship process, so you will be prepared when the time comes.

STEP TWO: VISIT COLLEGES

Visiting a college is the final, critical step in choosing where your child will attend. You can't really tell the personality of a college from their brochures, or professionals at a college fair. Even if a school has the word "Christian" in their name and has a Christian representative at a fair, that doesn't mean they share your family's values. Names mean nothing. A quick Google search for "Texas Christian University Top 10 Party

Schools" explains why the college visit is a crucial ingredient to successfully launching your child. Four years is a long time! They could live at college for four years of their life, so visiting is vitally important in the process of choosing. These tips will help you make the most of your time.

Compare College Statistics

Before you visit a college in person, it can help to compare statistics. I used books; US News, Barron's, and Peterson's. They all look about the same – like a huge, big city phone book. Like a phone book, you don't have to read every page, you only read the portions you need.

Compare all these books while you're at the library, and jot down notes. If you don't have the time or inclination, then I would stick with the one by US News. It's the best known of the three

For each college you have in mind, though, read every single word about it in those books. Some of the details are tiny but hugely important. Of course you are looking for the majors they offer, and housing, but it's more than just that. You want to know how much the average child pays (or gets in scholarships) and then see if your child compares in terms of the SAT or ACT scores. You want to know how many years it takes the average student to graduate. You want to know what percent are employed when they graduate – and what percent get into graduate school.

Official Visit

No matter whether you will be visiting on a day when hundreds of other potential students are visiting, or just touring on your own, make sure the admissions department knows you're coming. They pay attention when students show interest in them, and you want them to know you're interested. Most college websites give you the opportunity to register for a visit, so don't miss the opportunity to let them know you're coming.

Meet the Staff

Since it's important to find a college who will love you just as much as you love them, make sure your student dresses neatly and is at their most charming during the visit. When you meet with representatives, resist the urge to jump in and run the show; back off and let your student do most of the interacting. That way, the college will get to know your child better, and get a better picture of who they are, beyond their application. Of course, it's entirely appropriate for parents to ask questions about homeschool records, etc., but let your child do most of the talking at this point.

Take a Tour

Don't miss the chance to have them attend a class or two. This will help them get a better idea of what day-to-day classes will be like. Also try to meet with a department head if your child has some idea of what they'd like to major in. Tours are usually offered too, so go check out the campus. Don't forget to take notes, so when your student writes their application essays, they can include details about their visit.

Go with Your Gut

Pay close attention when you visit, using all your senses. What is your intuition saying? Is it a whisper, or a shout? What is your initial gut instinct? Is this a positive environment? Can you see your child living here for four years?

Look Closely

Pay attention to what you see on campus. Are the students happy? Is this a pleasant place to be? What do the grounds look like? If the place is worn and littered, it might indicate the students don't take much pride in their school. Also ask specific questions about what happens on campus, such as special events, resources, etc. Just like at many institutions, this kind of information is often posted on the walls of the bathrooms, so make sure to check that out! Do the activities seem fun? Are they consistent with your values? I remember one college my husband and I visited that had so many fun activities, we wished we could attend!

Listen Carefully

In addition to looking, make sure to listen too. What are the student and faculty conversations like? Are people respectful? Is their conversation laced with profanity? Listening to professors can tell you a lot about a school, too: do they know their students by name? Talk to them as adults? Do they seem like good role models for your child?

Taste the Food

Most colleges will provide prospective families with a free voucher to use in the campus dining hall. Eating the food during a visit is a MUST! Your child will be eating here for at least several years, three times a day, seven days a week! And if your child has any kind of food allergies, the college must be able to accommodate them.

Clean Environment

Lastly, pay attention to whether the

school is clean. It doesn't have to be spotless, but is it consistent with your family standards? More importantly, how does the environment make you feel about safety and security? Is this a place your child will enjoy and feel comfortable living in?

Overnight Visits

Once you have narrowed your search to just a few colleges, have your child spend a night on campus, and experience life in the dorms. This is their opportunity to get to know the student population a little better, and if they live on campus, a huge proportion of their time will be spent in the dorms. Most schools offer this opportunity, and it's another chance to demonstrate to them how serious you are about their school!

Thank You Note

After a college visit, it's important to send thank you notes to the admissions staff and any professors you spent time with. Both parents and students can do this, and both email and snail mail are appropriate. If you are really interested in a college, I recommend sending both.

STEP THREE: CHOOSE SOME COLLEGES

After you have visited colleges, you might have a much better idea which colleges will be a good fit for your child. Applying to reach, fit, and safety colleges can help prevent heartache.

Reach, Fit, and Safety Colleges

How do you choose a wide variety of colleges? You compare your student's test scores to the colleges' test scores. A 'reach' college is one where the average test scores are higher than your child's, yet your child will meet their expectations. A 'fit' college is where the average test score is about the same as your child's test scores, and your child meets their expectations. A 'safety' school is where their test scores are actually below your child's test scores, and your child will exceed their expectations. This is one of the reasons why you want to know your child's test scores ahead of time. That's why the PSAT, the SAT, and the ACT are important in junior year – the information will help you choose reach, fit, and safety schools.

Of course, it's not all about the test scores. Those scores are really just estimates, but they can help you figure out where you fit in the wide range of colleges out there.

Keep in mind that Ivy League schools, military academies and other extremely selective schools like MIT are always reach schools, no matter what your test scores are.

Choose Colleges for Application

There are a huge variety of colleges out there, and some of them will look very similar to each other, so it's very difficult to know where you should apply. Once you've figured that out, you need to remember the application process is quite long, and I recommend you start on the very first day of senior year. That means you need to know where you want to apply by the end of junior year.

Choose a wide variety of colleges to apply to, including private colleges and state universities. I have heard on average, most children apply to eight colleges. Four to twelve is a common number of colleges to apply to.

When you apply to a variety of schools, you're almost sure to find a perfect fit that will accept you, and may provide great scholarships. Using the information you have obtained, choose at least four colleges where your child can apply. You want them to apply to this many schools, so you can ensure some success with admission and scholarship.

My book, "The HomeScholar's Guide to College Admission and Scholarships" is a great place to start learning about this process. It's available in paperback and on Kindle, and covers all the topics necessary for college success, including how to search for colleges and interpret college statistics, how to visit the colleges and evaluate what you discover, and how to receive merit-based scholarships and market students effectively to the colleges of their choice.

Find out more about the book here:

www.TheHomeScholar.com/
CollegeAdmissionBook

Chapter 6

Facing the Community College Fad

When I speak to groups, I sometimes express my dissatisfaction with dual enrollment in community college. Extremely popular with homeschoolers, I often get asked why I am hesitant about such programs and the current trend.

"Rated R" Environment

In my own experience, and in talking with many other parents, I have concluded that community college is often a "Rated R" environment. Even with careful control of the curriculum and selection of the teachers, it is still an "adult" situation.

Professors at these schools have told me

they use the "sex sells" approach. In a high school, although there are many issues, there are generally limits to the use of inappropriate material to sell their educational product. There are no such limits in a community college. Community colleges are meant to be an adult environment. They cater to the broad expanse of adults, not the unique subset of homeschool young adults who don't want to mix education with unrelated material.

Community college will provide the socialization you normally see in a public high school. Because they are public institutions, community colleges come complete with all the "public school" worldview and academics - which is often the reason many homeschoolers avoid public school in the first place.

I know I have a unique perspective on community college, and I don't think for a minute that my view is right and others are wrong. Community college is a current fad in homeschooling, and my job is to provide information. I want to provide both sides of the full story so parents can make a wise choice based on what they know about their own children. Armed with this knowledge you can avoid the lemming mentality, and make choices with your eyes wide open.

Parents are the best qualified to make these choices, and my job is to open the discussion. I see parents feeling pressured to put their children into dual enrollment in high school. I'm trying to remove that pressure, so people can make judgments based on their understanding of the situation, and not do it just because other people are doing it.

Our Community College Stories

My children attended community college for one year, during their last year before the university. These are our experience with a local community college.

- The student bookstore sold pornographic magazines next to the engineering textbooks.
- The calculus professor dropped the f-bomb in every sentence. We were able to choose a different professor

who was a homeschool graduate. He even came to our own graduation celebration, and he wrote a fabulous letter of recommendation for my children.

- The physics professor used marital positions to describe physics principles. As luck would have it, we were assigned to a different professor.
- In the Music Improvisation class the books said, "I capitalize the word 'Self' because I was taught to capitalize the name of God, and only God can create music." The class included a mantra each day, "I am Good, I am Great, I am God." We declined to take that class.
- The French teacher showed movies with unclothed people to demonstrate the culture.
- The speech teacher and the curriculum were great, but one of the other students did a speech on the religion of sex, which was a bit too eye-opening for my teens.
- The Political Science class was taught by a self-proclaimed Marxist.

My students were well prepared for college. Within the first 2 weeks of community college, they had done all the reading and completed all the assignments they could. They spent the remaining 6 weeks learning how to do nothing and get A's without trying.

We couldn't find many classes that would challenge my sons and at the same time not offend our faith. My political science aficionado ended up taking only engineering science and math classes. I'm certainly glad he was able to tolerate differential equations!

On the bright side, the community college did have an honors program. With additional coursework you could get "honors" with each course. That seemed to help the academic level slightly, but it still did not bring it up to the difficulty level of our homeschool.

We noticed that for the first time, my children encountered people who didn't want to learn. Some students felt a 0.7 GPA was a passing grade and receiving a 2.0 in a class was "good." Many students didn't show up for class, or didn't participate in classroom discussion even when they knew the answer.

I go to a lot of college fairs. One community college representative took me aside and said, "Please tell homeschoolers not to send their children to community college! We have adjudicated people in the classes!" She said felons and registered offenders were known to be on campus, and she worried about innocent homeschoolers. I'm sure the criminal element is relatively rare (although how would we know?) but the point is still important.

Stories from Other Moms

"My daughter just started attending the local community college this week. Already she has an assignment from her Art Appreciation professor that has me wondering what colleges are teaching these days. *rolling eyes*"

"A piece of paper was passed around the class with a list of two items to compare. They were to choose one set and write a paper. My daughter saw the word "chapel" and picked it, although she didn't know what the other word was."

"We now know it's a series of "art" films. She and I have seen the trailer, and both of us have found it to be offensive. The whole movie was bizarre representations of the reproductive systems. Plus, there were some gruesome death scenes too. We saw all this during just the 5 minute trailer!"

"She's said that she's going to talk with her professor about picking a different group to compare. I pray the teacher is understanding and won't give my daughter a hard time. I know "art" is subjective, but SHEESH!"
~ Jen in Texas

Jen was extremely surprised this could happen at a community college in her area, because they live in a conservative Bible-belt region.

Being forewarned is not enough. Linda heard me speak at a College Fair and was well aware of the risks. Last fall she sent me this note,

> "Two weeks into our 16 year old daughter's first quarter at community college, two pornographic reading assignments were handed out in her required English class. I knew from prior discussions with you that dual enrollment was risky. However, I thought if we were "selective" in the classes we took, we could avoid the problems you had warned me about. We are looking for alternatives at this time."
> ~Linda in Washington

Now her daughter is faced with a permanent academic record that may include a withdrawal or failing grade, and the parents are considering their next steps.

It's not Naiveté

I do not believe the experience at community college is only a problem with very young students, and I don't believe it has anything to do with naiveté in general. One mom who returned to community college wrote in her blog:

> "There are no morals, no discipline, and evolution and political correctness reigns supreme. The students in the classes were very disrespectful. I could not believe how much they mouthed off to the teachers. In my algebra class, students would say, "I hate your teaching." "You are the worst teacher." etc. In speech class, one student offered to pay for the exam ahead of time. Cheating was rampant. If you want to pass without studying, I suppose it's possible. Students were programming answers in their calculators, getting up to "go to the bathroom" during the exams, and the math teacher even left the classroom while we were taking an

exam!"

"As far as sending your kids to these colleges, all I can say is you better be sure your child is real grounded in the Word. That they have more than a head knowledge of God and they are determined to live by His principles. If not, you are sending your child into a war zone without weapons. It was bad in my day (1960s) but today, it's unbelievably worse. In the 60s, at least there were some morals left. Today, there are none. I was talking with one little girl who was programming her calculator with answers to the Algebra quiz. She offered to program mine since I didn't know how to do it. When I said that I couldn't sleep at night if I did that, she answered very sincerely, "It's not really cheating. I'm only taking this course because it's required. It's different if it's your major." She was sincere in her answer and believed that that was ok!"

~Cindy Downes, My First Exposé of College, collegeat57.wordpress.com

Cindy is neither a young student, nor is she naive, and yet she had issues and unique difficulties. The stories we hear about homeschoolers going to college are the same stories we would hear if our adult friends were going to community college. It's not the children, it's the environment.

Another mother reported her local Christian college does not accept community college writing courses at all. They believe community college English courses involve topics that are much too controversial for high school students. This university responded to the community college environment by rejecting all such college credits. Although this is unusual, it's best to check with the university your child hopes to eventually attend, so you aren't disappointed.

Community college mixes the best and brightest students with those who struggle the most – and puts them in the same class.

One website explains: "Our Honors and

Early College/Dual Enrollment programs attract some of the best and brightest minds. Our open-door policies allow students who need remediation to get the skills they need for college-level courses" www.fldoe.org/cc/. Two such varied situations, two sentences side by side, representing two students sitting next to each other in class. It can be difficult for either child in that situation.

Public universities will often (not always) have higher academic expectations, and the students population will often have higher academic expectations. Community college students are frequently remedial in one way or another. The students are often not ready for a university – financially, academically, socially, or for some other reason. That means they can be a challenge to educate, which makes it a unique educational setting.

I asked my son if he thought community college had been a mistake. At the age of 20 he said "YES!" If I could do my life over again, I would have not done dual enrollment. I would have either continued homeschooling and achieved outside documentation through testing, or I would have graduated them a year early and sent them to a Christian University where the cultural and academic clash would have been less severe.

Is Community College Right for your Family?

Ask your local friends about their community college experiences. They may start with the positives. When you talk to parents who have gone before, they will say things like, "We had a wonderful experience but...." Listen for the "But...." If you had heard that disclaimer about a public high school, would you be tempted to enroll your child?

Think deeply about your feelings about public and secular universities. If you would not want your child to go to a public university or if you are concerned about the values at a private university, then community college will not be a good fit. One parent enrolled her children in community college and then explained, "My husband and I think college is not worth the money and what kids are taught in college is questionable. If they choose to go to college, the school will be carefully chosen." Consider that if a university is not a good fit for moral or religious reasons, then perhaps a community college is unlikely to fit your family either.

If you choose to send your child, there are some strategies that may mitigate trouble. Find a support group of like-minded individuals, either homeschoolers or Christian groups who meet regularly. Utilize the "buddy system" and keep your kids in class with another homeschooler. Carefully read all online comments about the professor on "RateMyProfessor.com." Preview the textbooks before the first day of class.

Alternatives to Community College

Community college can be great outside documentation of academics, but there are alternatives. You can provide test scores instead, using SAT, ACT, SAT Subject Tests, CLEP and AP. You can provide letters of recommendation through internships and apprenticeships. You can also homeschool some college using online courses or credit by examination.

When you are considering community college, don't be naive and think it will be a perfect educational utopia. Be aware that it may be more "Rated R" than your student is ready for. If the crowd seems to all follow the community college route, that doesn't mean you have to follow along yourself. Consider carefully, know your child, and trust your own judgment.

Chapter 7

Get a Jump on Senior Year

If you want to make junior year really successful, the best thing is to get a jump on senior year. Don't ignore the college admission process that is nearly upon you.

Assume the colleges where your student plans to apply will need course descriptions and start creating them. You'd be surprised at how many people call me in the late fall of senior year and say they need their course descriptions and transcripts by the following morning! You really need to plan ahead for those, because it's very difficult to make it happen overnight. One of the best things you can do during junior year is to make sure all of your course descriptions and your transcripts are up to date.

Work on finding some college scholarships during junior year as well. A lot of them are available to high school juniors, and you can use that writing for your English credit.

English Class Suggestions

During junior year, you can teach some college application skills for English credit. If you grab some applications when you're at the college fair, you can practice application essays using those essay topics. You can practice the pre-writing, drafting, editing, and revising. It's really good practice, and you can use those application essays for topics.

Occasionally, a high school senior will put their foot down and you just can't get them to write application essays. If you've already practiced during junior year, it's a lot easier to convince your child to dust off something they've already written, and just spruce it up a little bit, than it is to write something from scratch. Even though those application essays are really great practice during junior year, they can save your bacon if you encounter some attitude problems in senior year.

You can also practice writing for AP exams. If you're taking an AP exam in English literature, all of the essays your child writes as they practice for the test can actually become part of their English credit. Those essays can also replace their other daily writing assignments.

Remember that test preparation includes reading and writing, and those are skills you use for English. It can replace other workbooks you've used as well. In addition, have your student practice filling out those college applications, not just the essays. This is good practice for filling out job applications, so I find that very helpful.

Search for Private Scholarships

Junior year is the time to start looking for private scholarships, and the best place to find them is online. However, you can't just search on the word "scholarship" on

Google, because you will come up with 3.8 million hits, which isn't very effective. It's better to find scholarships by using scholarship search engines. The one I recommend is Fastweb.com, since I find it the easiest to use.

Filter the scholarships that come up in your search. This will quickly eliminate as many bad-fit scholarships as possible. The first time a scholarships says it's "for public school students only," don't get angry and waste a lot of time wondering why they won't let private school kids or homeschoolers apply. Just delete it off your list and move on to the next one.

After you have filtered through the scholarships, organize them by due date, so that you can turn them in on time. It doesn't matter how perfect a fit the scholarship is if you turn it in late!

Follow-through is by far the most difficult part of scholarship work, because your student has to do this part, not you. They must make time to actually do the work of writing or completing the required project. For example, a thousand word essay is not something most kids can usually pull together in an hour, so they must set aside time to do this.

After your student has worked hard and submitted their scholarships, make sure to file or include that experience on their transcript. You can add their projects to your course descriptions—if they have done something that would be part of an English topic, include it in their English class course description. If they wrote an essay, then of course you could count it towards an English credit, but sometimes scholarships call for something else, such as making a YouTube video, in which case you could include it as part of a technology course description.

If your student is commended for something, make sure you add it to their awards list too. This can really help build up their awards list, even if it isn't a really significant award.

Scholarships do take quite a bit of time. It takes time to complete the project or the assignment, and to complete the application that goes with the scholarship. However, if you really need financial assistance, then searching for private scholarships during junior year can be a helpful thing.

If you are very serious about scholarship money, there is one financial consideration I will share. I'm not a financial advisor, so you want to talk to your financial advisor about this. However, a lot of scholarships from colleges are tied to the income of the parent, and they make that determination based on your income beginning January 1 of junior year. That means when your child is a junior, they start counting your income starting January 1, and then count it for a whole year.

If you really need a lot of financial aid, one of the things you can do is to maximize your retirement savings during junior year, in order to make your income appear lower. All of a sudden, you look like you have more financial need, and you may get more financial aid. At the same time, you're saving more money for your retirement. It benefits you in the long run and it prioritizes your needs, as well. It doesn't need to always be about our children. It can also be about us and our retirement savings. So if you haven't started saving for college and you have a junior, January 1 of junior year is an excellent time for you to boost your retirement savings.

College Expectations

It's important to determine the expectations of the colleges, and meet or exceed those expectations when you can. If a school requires certain classes like biology and chemistry, then you want to find that out.

Also find out if they require subject tests like an AP or SAT 2, or want validation or extra tests. Some colleges will prefer the ACT instead of the SAT and you want to give them what they want. Sometimes they will want a homeschool student to have taken some community college courses. Sometimes colleges will accept some online classes as a way for them to have outside documentation. The point is to make sure you know what the school is looking for, what their expectations are, and then exceed those expectations so your student looks fabulous!

Life Skills

Another way to get a jump on senior year is to make sure you teach your child life skills so they'll be ready for college when it comes. Prepare your children for independent living, which includes such things as cooking, cleaning, laundry, banking, and the importance of sleep.

Also careful they don't spend too much time on technology. Help them to develop a good work ethic, to learn from their failures, and to become more and more independent, so when college arrives, they will be equipped not just to survive, but to thrive!

Appendix 1

Take the PSAT for Fun and Profit

I was at my husband's softball game doing what I love doing at his games - talking about homeschooling, when my friend Kathy said to me, "I never took the PSAT in high school. I don't think I knew anything about it. Suddenly all my friends were taking it one weekend, and by then it was too late to sign up!"

Some things never change! Every year I talk to students who are in the same situation Kathy had been in decades ago. They don't realize the test is available, or that they need to register. The next thing they know, they are spending the day alone, while all their friends are taking the test.

In this section, you will learn the two purposes of the PSAT, how homeschoolers can take the test, and what the benefits are. The PSAT is only offered once a year, so it's really easy to miss. The ONLY way to make sure your student can take the test is to plan ahead. Sound intimidating? I'll break the information down into bite-sized pieces.

The complete name for the test is PSAT/NMSQT which stands for Preliminary SAT National Merit Scholarship Qualifying Test. Don't just think "Wow! That's the biggest acronym I've ever seen!" The name can help you decipher the two functions of the PSAT.

The first name, PSAT means it's a practice test that you can take "for fun" to learn about the SAT. The second name, NMSQT means National Merit Scholarship Qualifying Test, which means you can take the test "for profit" as a junior. Either way can benefit your student. Let me describe the functions of the PSAT so you feel completely comfortable with it.

First Name of the PSAT/NMSQT

The first name of the test is PSAT. It's the portion of the test that is the preliminary, practice, or pre-SAT. You can take the test for practice in tenth or eleventh grade. I call this "take the test for fun!" because your scores don't matter. The results are just for you, with no negative repercussions at all. You can use it as a starting point, before you study for the SAT. It is also used to estimate your SAT scores.

The PSAT provides firsthand practice for the SAT. It measures reading, writing, and math. Each section is given a score of 20 to 80, with about 50 being an average score. When you get the results, add a zero to the score of each section, and that will estimate your score for the SAT. For example, if you get a 62 in the PSAT reading, it is likely you will get around 620 in reading on the SAT. When you get the score results, they will tell you what score range you are likely to have on the SAT, which will help you find a college that can match your academic rigor.

The PSAT also provides practice in taking standardized fill-in-the-bubble tests in a really challenging environment. In a sea of germs, surrounded by tattoos, body piercings, and smelly teenagers, my sons sat in alphabetical order in a public school cafeteria. Certainly not perfect conditions for a test, but it was definitely good to experience the setting of the SAT before the test counted! Taking a timed test around strangers is difficult. It's more difficult when you haven't practiced it first. The PSAT can provide practice in taking a test in "less than perfect" non-homeschooling conditions.

"Comparative" Function of the PSAT

One of the few drawbacks of homeschooling is we sometimes lack a sense of where our students fit within the norm. Taking the PSAT for fun will give you a percentile score, which compares your student against other bright college-bound students of the same age. We know perfectly well the foibles of our students and their weak areas, but we often don't realize exactly how smart they are compared to the rest of the gene pool. This test can be a startling reminder of how efficient and effective homeschooling can be! Even struggling learners in a homeschool environment will often test average or above in standardized tests that compare them to other college-bound high school students.

The comparative function will also give you a helpful "data point" about your student if they simply do not test well. Nobody is perfect, and of course there are students who won't test well even though they may be quite bright. Taking the PSAT for fun, without the risk of negative repercussions, can help you determine whether to use standardized test scores at all when applying to college.

If your student does very poorly on the test, you can decide to use other tools at your disposal to document your homeschool achievement. Based on the "for fun" score, you could decide to submit a portfolio instead of a test score. You might also decide to take community college courses to prove college readiness. More options will be available when you have the information from this test.

The test is good for comparison because it's standardized - and that means states requiring a test from homeschoolers will often accept the PSAT. Better still, this is a very inexpensive test, so you can save money if you use this test over some others. As far as tests go, the PSAT is a pretty cheap way to meet your state's requirement for annual testing.

"College Search" Function of the PSAT

Check the yes box beside Student Search Service in the "About the Student" section before you begin the test. This will allow colleges to see information about your student - and you'll be well on your way to starting your college search. That's good because colleges will start marketing to your student. You can find out about perfect fit colleges you otherwise wouldn't have considered. Yours could be the student they want! They may be looking for a homeschooled student in Oregon who wants to be a doctor, or maybe they would take ANY student from North

Dakota, just so they can get another state represented at their school. The student search can tell you which colleges want YOU. By the end of junior year, you should know which colleges you want to apply to, and having interested colleges mailing you information can really help.

The Second Name of the PSAT/NMSQT

You can also take this test "for profit!" The second name of the test is the National Merit Scholarship Qualifying Test (NMSQT). Although people rarely refer to the test by its second name, it's the part of the test that's "for profit."

If you have heard of some students becoming a "National Merit Scholar" or "National Merit Commended Student," the NMSQT is how they were chosen. It's national because everyone can take it, even homeschoolers. It measures academic merit, meaning a good score and quality academics will get you considered for the scholarship. It's a scholarship, because students who earn the National Merit Scholarship are awarded financial aid for college. – $2500 per year or more. And it's a qualifying test because it's just the beginning of the scholarship process – first you take the test, and then there are other hoops to jump through, which may lead to other scholarships.

Only juniors can take the PSAT "For Profit." Although 10th and 11th graders can take the test "for fun," only juniors in high school will have their score count for the NMSQT function of the test. Otherwise the test is just for fun. Taking the PSAT during sophomore year does not count toward the national merit scholarship.

Since the PSAT is a practice test for the SAT, it can be "for profit" even if you don't win the scholarship. College financial aid is often tied to SAT scores, and anything you do to raise your score can save you thousands of dollars.

Raising your score can be as easy as practice, practice, practice. The PSAT is the test that most closely resembles the SAT. It has the same environment, the same kids, the same noises, sights, and smells as the real test. Using this as a practice test can really save you money on college.

Register for the Test

Schools sometimes register kids in June, before classes end for summer. Other schools register for the test during the first week of school. It's fairly easy to access as a homeschooler, but you must be mindful of the registration deadline, as it is early in the school year. Find more information at www.collegeboard.org.

Find a school first, then call them right away. The test is only held once each year, and it's easy to miss if you put off the call. Here is what the College Board says: "If you are a home-schooled student, contact a principal or counselor at a local public or independent high school to make arrangements to take the PSAT/NMSQT at their school. Be sure to do so well in advance of the mid-October test dates, preferably during the previous June."

Learn about the Test

The PSAT is simply a measurement of reading, writing, and math. You can bring a calculator, and the math section includes algebra and geometry. Consequently, taking the test "for fun" may not be much fun without having some algebra and geometry under your belt.

The test is quite long, but it takes longer than you'd expect because of breaks between sections. As I mentioned earlier, each section of the test is graded on a crazy, 20 to 80 scale. Generally speaking, a score of about 50 is average, 60 is good, 70 is great, and 80 is perfect.

I only rarely suggest you should have your child study for the PSAT. Instead, I like to think of it as being the "starting point" for studying for the SAT. But for some students it might make sense to study for this test. If your child has a good chance to get the National Merit, for example, then studying for the PSAT might be the little bit they need to join the "in" crowd.

For an anxious student, some practice may help them feel comfortable with the "process" of testing. If you are interested in studying for the test, there are options. If you register with Petersons.com, you can get one free online sample test. You can also find PSAT test prep books from REA and Princeton Review.

You will also get one free Official Student Guide to the PSAT when you register for the test at the school, and it includes a sample test. Make sure you read the guide, because there is a lot of information in there that will help you.

Make sure your student fills out the student information section as well. They will be asked questions about what classes they have taken in high school. Since homeschoolers rarely talk about that sort of thing with our students, sometimes kids don't have a clue what courses they have taken, or what grades mom intends to give them.

What should you do right now? What do you do with this information? If you have a 9th grader, go to your calendar now.

Write "Register for PSAT" during the first week of June. If you have a 10th grader, decide if they should take the test for fun this year. Put it on your calendar for June if you want them to take it again next year. If you have an 11th grader, register for the test quickly, and put the October test date on your calendar.

Missed the PSAT?

Don't beat yourself up! Just make sure your student takes the SAT or ACT as soon as possible. Here are two links to help you learn more about those tests: SAT (www.collegeboard.org) and ACT (www.act.org.)

In a public school setting, there are advisors and counselors. They are each assigned hundreds of students. You know how hard it is to get our teenagers to do things sometimes? They have that same trouble in public schools! There are many kids in high schools who don't pay attention to their advisor and don't sign up for the test. They forget, delay, and don't pay attention in a public school as well. If you can get your kids to the PSAT, that's great! If not, don't think a public school would do a better job of advising. Parents are the best advisers, because we have more at stake. These aren't just "kids." These are OUR kids! And that makes all the difference!

Scheduled for the PSAT?

Here are some test tips to help things go smoothly.

A Few Days Before

- Go over the whole test booklet. The kids will need detailed instructions, so explain and review before the test
- Take one practice test, preferably using a timer
- Tell the kids you can't get 100% on this test, they just need to do their best

One Day Before the Test

- Don't bother with test prep, test prep is relaxation at this point
- Pack at least 4 sharp pencils, a familiar calculator, water or juice,

and small snack
- Get a good night's sleep

Morning of the Test

- Start with a good breakfast complete with protein
- Show up with the PSAT Homeschool Code
- Have the student locate the bathroom
- Turn off their cell phone completely
- Determine a place to meet after the test

After the Test

- Celebrate successful completion and take them out for ice cream or a meal
- Remind them you can't get 100% on this test, so everyone feels like they didn't do so well

The PSAT is a good idea for a sophomore and junior in high school. It can help them practice for the college admission tests, so they don't feel anxious. Tell them the scores don't matter, and encourage them to relax. This is just an opportunity to see what it's like to fill in a bubble test with 100 of their neighbors.

Some homeschoolers have developed a concern about public high school, because the only time they think about it is when there is a shooting or assault in the news. Help them to relax and feel safe. We don't have to approve of the public school environment, but our children can still be encouraged to relax when they visit for the test.

Afterword

Who is Lee Binz, and What Can She Do for Me?

Number one best-selling homeschool author, Lee Binz is The HomeScholar. Her mission is "helping parents homeschool high school." Lee and her husband Matt homeschooled their two boys, Kevin and Alex, from elementary through high school.

Upon graduation, both boys received four-year, full tuition scholarships from their first choice university. This enables Lee to pursue her dream job - helping parents homeschool their children through high school.

On The HomeScholar website, you'll find great products for creating homeschool transcripts and comprehensive records to help you amaze and impress colleges.

Find out why Andrew Pudewa, Director at Institute for Excellence in Writing says: "Lee Binz knows how to navigate this often confusing and frustrating labyrinth better than anyone."

You can find Lee online at:

www.TheHomeScholar.com

If this book has been helpful, could you please take a minute to write us a quick review on Amazon?

Thank you!

Testimonials

"Lee,

Just thought I would drop a line and let you know how thankful I am for all of your wonderful wisdom. The other day I had sat down to work on my son's transcripts when it dawned on me... **YOU have made it possible, for my gifted child to be able to do his transcripts** and course descriptions, himself.

What a fantastic opportunity for him to read, listen and learn. After all, it is ALL about him. By the end of his high school experience he will have learned enough to be able to communicate clearly to the colleges what he has been preparing for.

If they have a question he will know the answer! Thank you again, for all you do! ~

~Virginia in Arkansas

"My oldest son, Adam, just graduated and is going to be attending Auburn University this fall with scholarships that will more than equal a full ride!! The information from your website, blogs, Gold Care Club, webinars and DVD's have been very helpful for us in planning for high school and college! Whenever I am asked questions about doing high school at home, I generally always direct people to check out your website."

~Andrea and her son Adam

For more information about my **Gold Care Club**, go to:

www.TheHomeScholar.com/gold-care.php

Also From
The HomeScholar...

- The HomeScholar Guide to College Admission and Scholarships: Homeschool Secrets to Getting Ready, Getting In and Getting Paid (Book and Kindle Book)
- Setting the Records Straight - How to Craft Homeschool Transcripts and Course Descriptions for College Admission and Scholarships (Book and Kindle Book)
- Preparing to Homeschool High School (DVD)
- Finding a College (DVD)
- The Easy Truth About Homeschool Transcripts (Kindle Book)
- Parent Training A la Carte (Online Training)

- Total Transcript Solution (Online Training, Tools and Templates)
- Comprehensive Record Solution (Online Training, Tools and Templates)
- Gold Care Club (Comprehensive Online Support and Training)
- Homeschool "Convention at Home" Kit (Book, DVDs and Audios)

The HomeScholar "Coffee Break Books" Released or Coming Soon on Kindle and Paperback:

- Delight Directed Learning: Guiding Your Homeschooler Toward Passionate Learning
- Creating Transcripts for Your Unique Child: Help Your Homeschool Graduate Stand Out from the Crowd
- Beyond Academics: Preparation for College and for Life
- Planning High School Courses: Charting the Course Toward High School Graduation
- Graduate Your Homeschooler in Style: Make Your Homeschool Graduation Memorable
- Keys to High School Success: Get Your Homeschool High School Started Right!

- Getting the Most Out of Your Homeschool This Summer: Learning just for the Fun of it!
- Finding a College: A Homeschooler's Guide to Finding a Perfect Fit
- College Scholarships for High School Credit: Learn and Earn With This Two-for-One Strategy!
- College Admission Policies Demystified: Understanding Homeschool Requirements for Getting In
- A Higher Calling: Homeschooling High School for Harried Husbands (by Matt Binz, Mr. HomeScholar)
- Gifted Education Strategies for Every Child: Homeschool Secrets for Success
- College Application Essays: A Primer for Parents
- Creating Homeschool Balance: Find Harmony Between Type A and Type Zzz...
- Homeschooling the Holidays: Sanity Saving Strategies and Gift Giving Ideas
- Your Goals this Year: A Year by Year Guide to Homeschooling High School
- Making the Grades: A Grouch-Free Guide to Homeschool Grading
- High School Testing: Knowledge That Saves Money

- Getting the BIG Scholarships: Learn Expert Secrets for Winning College Cash!
- Easy English for Simple Homeschooling: How to Teach, Assess and Document High School English
- Scheduling - The Secret to Homeschool Sanity: Plan You Way Back to Mental Health
- Junior Year is the Key to Homeschool Success: How to Unlock the Gate to Graduation and Beyond
- Upper Echelon Education: How to Gain Admission to Elite Universities
- How to Homeschool College: Save Time, Reduce Stress and Eliminate Debt
- Homeschool Curriculum That's Effective and Fun: Avoid the Crummy Curriculum Hall of Shame!
- Comprehensive Homeschool Records: Put Your Best Foot Forward to Win College Admission and Scholarships
- Options After High School: Steps to Success for College or Career
- How to Homeschool 9th and 10th Grade: Simple Steps for Starting Strong!

- Senior Year Step-by-Step: Simple Instructions for Busy Homeschool Parents

Would you like to be notified when we offer the next *Coffee Break Books* free or discounted during our Kindle promotion days? Leave your name and email below and we will send you a reminder.

http://www.TheHomeScholar.com/freekindlebook.php

Visit my Amazon Author Page!

amazon.com/author/leebinz

64712053R00059

Made in the USA
Lexington, KY
17 June 2017